BILL GATES BIOGRAPHY

by David Right

ALL COPYRIGHTS RESERVED 2017
All Rights Reserved

Copyright 2017 by David Right - All rights reserved.

This document is geared towards providing exact and reliable information in regards to the topic and issue covered. The publication is sold with the idea that the publisher is not required to render accounting, officially permitted, or otherwise, qualified services. If advice is necessary, legal or professional, a practiced individual in the profession should be ordered.

- From a Declaration of Principles which was accepted and approved equally by a Committee of the American Bar Association and a Committee of Publishers and Associations.

In no way is it legal to reproduce, duplicate, or transmit any part of this document in either electronic means or in printed format. Recording of this publication is strictly prohibited and any storage of this document is not allowed unless with written permission from the publisher. All rights reserved.

The information provided herein is stated to be truthful and consistent, in that any liability, in terms of inattention or otherwise, by any usage or abuse of any policies, processes, or directions contained within is the solitary and utter responsibility of the recipient reader. Under no circumstances will any legal responsibility or blame be held against the publisher for any reparation, damages, or monetary loss due to the information herein, either directly or indirectly.

Respective authors own all copyrights not held by the publisher.

The information herein is offered for informational purposes solely, and is universal as so. The presentation of the information is without contract or any type of guarantee assurance.

The trademarks that are used are without any consent, and the publication of the trademark is without permission or backing by the trademark owner. All trademarks and brands within this book are for clarifying purposes only and are the owned by the owners themselves, not affiliated with this document.

DEDICATION

PREFACE

Bill Gates- the man who introduced the world to Microsoft is the one of the best-known entrepreneurs of the world. More than Microsoft, Bill gates is better known for his money. The man held the title of the 'richest person in the world' for 15 years in a row. Even as of February 2008, bill stood to be the third richest person in the world.

At Microsoft, Bill gates worked as a CEO and a chief software architect. To date, Bill is the largest individual shareholder with more than 8 percent of the common stock. The business entrepreneur gave away the position of the CEO in January 2000. However, he continued to act as a non executive chairman for the company. He held part time responsibilities with Microsoft and took over full-time work at the Bill & Melinda Gates Foundation in June 2006.

Contents

ALL COPYRIGHTS RESERVED 2017 2

DEDICATION...4

PREFACE...5

CHAPTER 1- THE BIOGRAPHY OF BILL GATES....................................7

CHAPTER 2- EDUCATION AND MARRIAGE 23

CHAPTER 3- BILL GATES AND STEVE JOBS RELATIONSHIP 28

CHAPTER 4- BILL GATES INVENTIONS- TOP-GREATEST HITS AND MISSES.......34

CHAPTER 5- THINGS YOU DON'T KNOW ABOUT BILL GATES...........45

CONCLUSION 48

CHAPTER 1- THE BIOGRAPHY OF BILL GATES

Entrepreneur Bill Gates founded the world's largest software business, Microsoft, with Paul Allen, and subse□uently became one of the richest men in the world.

"Success is a lousy teacher. It seduces smart people into thinking they can't lose."
—Bill Gates

Synopsis

Born in Seattle, Washington, in 1955, famed entrepreneur Bill Gates began to show an interest in computer programming at age 13. Through technological innovation, keen business strategy and aggressive business tactics, he and partner Paul Allen built the world's largest software business, Microsoft. In the process, Gates became one of the richest men in the world. In February 2014, Gates announced that he was stepping down as Microsoft's chairman.

Early Life

Bill Gates was born William Henry Gates III on October 28, 1955, in Seattle, Washington. Gates began to show an interest in computer programming at the age of 13 at the Lakeside School. He pursued his passion through college. Striking out on his own with his friend and business partner Paul Allen, Gates found himself at the right place at the right time. Through technological innovation, keen business strategy and aggressive business tactics, he built the world's largest software business, Microsoft. In the process, Gates became one of the richest men in the world.

Bill Gates grew up in an upper middle-class family with two sisters: Kristianne, who is older, and Libby, who is younger. Their father, William H. Gates Sr., was a promising, if somewhat shy, law student when he met his future wife, Mary Maxwell. She was an athletic, outgoing student at the University of Washington, actively involved in student affairs and leadership. The Gates family atmosphere was warm and close, and all three children were encouraged to be competitive and strive for excellence. Bill showed early signs of competitiveness when he coordinated family athletic games at their summer house on Puget Sound. He also relished in playing board games (Risk was his favorite) and excelled at Monopoly.

Bill had a very close relationship with his mother, Mary, who after a brief career as a teacher devoted her time to helping raise the children and working on civic affairs and with charities. She also served on several corporate boards, including those of the First Interstate Bank in Seattle (founded by her grandfather), the United Way and International Business Machines (IBM). She would often take Bill along when she volunteered in schools and at community organizations.

Bill was a voracious reader as a child, spending many hours poring over reference books such as the encyclopedia. Around the age of 11 or 12, Bill's parents began to have concerns about his behavior. He was doing well in school, but he seemed bored and withdrawn at times, and his parents worried he might become a loner. Though they were strong believers in public education, when Bill turned 13, they enrolled him at Seattle's exclusive preparatory Lakeside School. He blossomed in nearly all his subjects, excelling in math and science, but also doing very well in drama and English.

While at Lakeside School, a Seattle computer company offered to provide computer time for the students. The Mother's Club used proceeds from the school's rummage sale to purchase a teletype terminal for students to use. Bill Gates became entranced with what a computer could do and spent much of his free time working on the terminal. He wrote a tic-tac-toe program in BASIC computer language that allowed users to play against the computer.

It was at Lakeside School that Bill met Paul Allen, who was two years his senior. The two became fast friends, bonding over their common enthusiasm for computers, even though they were very different people. Allen was more reserved and shy. Bill was feisty and at times combative. Regardless of their differences, they both spent much of their free time together working on programs. Occasionally, they disagreed and would clash over who was right or who should run the computer lab. On one occasion, their argument escalated to the point where Allen banned Gates from the computer lab. On another occasion, Gates and Allen had their school computer privileges revoked for taking advantage of software glitches to obtain free computer time from the company that provided the computers. After their probation, they were allowed back in the computer lab when they offered to debug the program. During this time, Gates developed a payroll program for the computer company the boys hacked into and a scheduling program for the school.

In 1970, at the age of 15, Bill Gates went into business with his pal, Paul Allen. They developed "Traf-o-Data," a computer program that monitored traffic patterns in Seattle, and netted $20,000 for their efforts. Gates and Allen wanted to start their own company, but Gates's parents wanted him to finish school and go on to college where they hoped he would work to become a lawyer.

Bill Gates graduated from Lakeside in 1973. He scored 1590 out of 1600 on the college SAT test, a feat of intellectual achievement that for several years he boasted about when introducing himself to new people.

Early Career

Gates enrolled at Harvard University in the fall, originally thinking of a career in law. But his freshman year saw him spend more of his time in the computer lab than in class. Gates did not really have a study regimen. Instead, he could get by on a few hours of sleep, cram for a test, and pass with a reasonable grade.

Gates remained in contact with Paul Allen, who, after attending Washington State University for two years, dropped out and moved to Boston, Massachusetts, to work for Honeywell. Around this time, Allen showed Gates an edition of Popular Electronics magazine featuring an article on the Altair 8800 mini-computer kit. Both boys were fascinated with the possibilities that this computer could create in the world of personal computing. The Altair was made by a small company in Albu□uer□ue, New Mexico, called Micro Instrumentation and Telemetry Systems (MITS). Gates and Allen contacted the company, proclaiming that they were working on a BASIC software program that would run the Altair computer. In reality, they didn't have an Altair to work with or the code to run it, but they wanted to know if MITS was interested in someone developing such software. MITS was, and its president, Ed Roberts, asked the boys for a demonstration. Gates and Allen scrambled, spending the next two months writing the software at Harvard's computer lab. Allen traveled to Albuquerque for a test run at MITS, never having tried it out on an Altair computer. It worked perfectly. Allen was hired at MITS, and Gates soon left Harvard to work with him, much to his parents' dismay. In 1975, Gates and Allen formed a partnership they called Micro-Soft, a blend of "micro-computer" and "software."

Microsoft (Gates and Allen dropped the hyphen in less than a year) started off on shaky footing. Though their BASIC software program for the Altair computer netted the company a fee and royalties, it wasn't meeting their overhead. Microsoft's BASIC software was popular with computer hobbyists, who obtained pre-market copies and were reproducing and distributing them for free. According to Gates's later account, only about 10 percent of the people using BASIC in the Altair computer had actually paid for it. At this time, much of the personal computer enthusiasts were people not in it for the money. They felt the ease of reproduction and distribution allowed them to share software with friends and fellow computer enthusiasts. Bill Gates thought differently. He saw the free distribution of software as stealing, especially when it involved software that was created to be sold.

In February 1976, Gates wrote an open letter to computer hobbyists, saying that continued distribution and use of software without paying for it would "prevent good software from being written." In essence, pirating software would discourage developers from investing time and money into creating quality software. The letter was unpopular with computer enthusiasts, but Gates stuck to his beliefs and would use the threat of innovation as a defense when faced with charges of unfair business practices.

Gates had a more acrimonious relationship with MITS president Ed Roberts, often resulting in shouting matches. The combative Gates clashed with Roberts on software development and the direction of the business. Roberts considered Gates spoiled and obnoxious. In 1977, Roberts sold MITS to another computer company and went back to Georgia to enter medical school and become a country doctor. Gates and

Allen were on their own. The pair had to sue the new owner of MITS to retain the software rights they had developed for Altair.

Microsoft wrote software in different formats for other computer companies, and, at the beginning of 1979, Gates moved the company's operations to Bellevue, Washington, just east of Seattle. Gates was glad to be home again in the Pacific Northwest, and threw himself into his work. All 25 employees of the young company had broad responsibilities for all aspects of the operation, product development, business development and marketing. With his acumen for software development and a keen business sense, Gates placed himself as the head of Microsoft, which grossed approximately $2.5 million in 1979. Gates was only 23.

The Rise of Microsoft

Gates's acumen for not only software development but also business operations put him in the position of leading the company and working as its spokesperson. He personally reviewed every line of code the company shipped, often rewriting code himself when he saw it necessary. As the computer industry began to grow with companies like Apple, Intel and IBM developing hardware and components, Bill was continuously out on the road touting the merits of Microsoft software applications. He often took his mother with him. Mary was highly respected and well connected with her membership on several corporate boards, including IBM's. It was through Mary that Bill Gates met the CEO of IBM.

In November 1980, IBM was looking for software that would operate their upcoming personal computer (PC) and approached Microsoft. Legend has it that at the first meeting with Bill Gates someone at IBM mistook him for an office assistant and asked him to serve coffee. Gates did look very young, but he quickly impressed IBM, convincing them that he and his company could meet their needs. The only problem was that Microsoft had not developed the basic operating system that would run IBM's new computers. Not to be stopped, Gates bought an operating system that was developed to run on computers similar to IBM's PC. He made a deal with the software's developer, making Microsoft the exclusive licensing agent and later full owner of the software but not telling them of the IBM deal. The company later sued Microsoft and Gates for withholding important information. Microsoft settled out of court for an undisclosed amount, but neither Gates nor Microsoft admitted to any wrongdoing.

Gates had to adapt the newly purchased software to work for the IBM PC. He delivered it for a $50,000 fee, the same price he had paid for the software in its original form. IBM wanted to buy the source code, which would have given them the information to the operating system. Gates refused, instead proposing that IBM pay a licensing fee for copies of the software sold with their computers. Doing this allowed Microsoft to license the software they called MS-DOS to any other PC manufacturer, should other computer companies clone the IBM PC, which they soon did. Microsoft also released software called Softcard, which allowed Microsoft BASIC to operate on Apple II machines.

Between 1979 and 1981, Microsoft's growth exploded, and staff increased from 25 to 128. Revenue also shot up from $2.5 million to $16 million. In mid-1981 Gates and Allen incorporated Microsoft, and Gates was appointed president and chairman of the board. Allen was named executive vice president.

By 1983, Microsoft was going global with offices in Great Britain and Japan, and with 30 percent of the world's computers running on its software. But 1983 also brought news that rocked Microsoft to its very foundation. Paul Allen was diagnosed with Hodgkin's disease. Though his cancer went into remission a year later with intensive treatment, Allen resigned from company that same year. Rumors abound as to why Allen left Microsoft. Some say Bill Gates pushed him out, but many say it was a life-changing experience for Allen and he saw there were other opportunities that he could invest his time in.

The Invention of Microsoft Windows

Though their rivalry is legend, Microsoft and Apple shared many of their early innovations. In 1981 Apple invited Microsoft to help develop software for Macintosh computers. Some developers were involved in both Microsoft development and the development of Microsoft applications for Macintosh. The collaboration could be seen in some shared names between the Microsoft and Macintosh systems.

It was through this knowledge sharing that Microsoft was to develop Windows, a system that used a mouse to drive a graphic interface, displaying text and images on the screen. This differed greatly from the text-and-keyboard driven MS-DOS system where all text formatting showed on the screen as code and not what actually would be printed. Bill Gates quickly recognized the threat this kind of software might pose for MS-DOS and Microsoft overall. For the unsophisticated user—which was most of the buying public—the graphic imagery of the competing VisiCorp software used in a Macintosh system would be so much easier to use. Gates announced in an advertising campaign that a new Microsoft operating system was about to be developed that would use a graphic interface. It was to be called "Windows," and would be compatible with all PC software products developed on the MS-DOS system. The announcement was a bluff, in that Microsoft had no such program under development. But as a marketing tactic, it was sheer genius as nearly 30 percent of the computer market was using the MS-DOS system and would wait for Windows software rather than change to a new system. Without people willing to change formats, software developers were unwilling to write programs for the VisiCorp system and it lost momentum by early 1985.

In November 1985, Bill Gates and Microsoft launched Windows; nearly two years after his announcement. Visually the Windows system looked very similar to the Macintosh system Apple Computer Corporation had introduced nearly two years earlier. Apple had earlier given Microsoft full access to their technology while it was working on making Microsoft products compatible for Apple computers. Gates had advised Apple to license their software but they ignored the advice, being more interested in selling computers. Once again, Gates took full advantage of the situation and created a software format that was strikingly similar to the Macintosh. Apple threatened to sue, and Microsoft retaliated, saying it would delay shipment of its Microsoft-compatible software for Macintosh users. In the end, Microsoft prevailed in the courts because it could prove that while there were similarities in how the two software systems operated, each individual function was distinctly different.

In March 1986, Bill Gates took Microsoft public with an initial public offering (IPO) of $21 per share. Gates held 45 percent of the company's 24.7 million shares and became an instant millionaire at age 31. Gates's stake at that time was $234 million of Microsoft's $520 million. Over time, the company's stock increased in value and split numerous times. In 1987, Bill Gates became a billionaire when the stock raised to $90.75 a share. Since then, Gates has been at the top, or at least near the top, of Forbes's annual list of the top 400 wealthiest people in America. In 1999, with stock prices at an all time high and the stock splitting eight-fold since its IPO, Gates's wealth briefly topped $101 billion.

Yet, Bill Gates never felt totally secure about the status of his company. Always having to look over his shoulder to see where the competition was, he developed a white-hot drive and competitive spirit. Gates expected everyone in the company to have the same dedication. One story of Gates's assistant coming to work early to find someone sleeping under a desk. She considered calling security or the police until she discovered it was Gates.

Bill Gates's intelligence allowed him to be able to see all sides of the software industry—product development and corporate strategy. When analyzing any corporate move, he would develop a profile of all the possible cases and run through them, asking questions about anything that could possibly happen. His confrontational management style became legend as he would challenge employees and their ideas to keep the creative process going. An unprepared presenter could hear, "That's the stupidest thing I've ever heard!" from Gates. But this was as much a test of the rigor of the employee as it was Gates's passion for his company. He was constantly checking the people around him to see if they were really convinced of their ideas.

Outside the company, Bill Gates was gaining a reputation as a ruthless competitor. Several tech companies, led by IBM, began to develop their own operating system, called OS/2, to replace MS-DOS. Rather than give in to the pressure, Gates pushed ahead with the Windows software, improving its operation and expanding its uses. In 1989, Microsoft introduced Microsoft Office, which bundled office productivity applications such as Microsoft Word and Excel into one system that was compatible with all Microsoft products. The applications were not as easily compatible with OS/2. Microsoft's new version of Windows sold 100,000 copies in just two weeks, and OS/2 soon faded away. This left Microsoft with a virtual monopoly on operating systems for PCs. Soon the

Federal Trade Commission began to investigate Microsoft for unfair marketing practices.

Throughout the 1990s, Microsoft faced a string of Federal Trade Commission and Justice Department investigations. Some related allegations that Microsoft made unfair deals with computer manufactures who installed the Windows operating system on their computers. Other charges involved Microsoft forcing computer manufactures to sell Microsoft's Internet Explorer as a condition for selling the Windows operating system with their computers.

At one point, Microsoft faced a possible break up of its two divisions—operating systems and software development. Microsoft defended itself, harking back to Bill Gates's earlier battles with software piracy and proclaiming that such restrictions were a threat to innovation. Eventually, Microsoft was able to find a settlement with the federal government to avoid a breakup. Through it all, Gates found some inventive ways to deflect the pressure with lighthearted commercials and public appearances at computer trade shows during which he posed as Star Trek's Mr. Spock. Gates continued to run the company and weather the federal investigations through the 1990s.

Personal Life

In 1987, a 23-year-old Microsoft product manager named Melinda French caught the eye of Bill Gates, then 32. The very bright and organized Melinda was a perfect match for Gates. In time, their relationship grew as they discovered an intimate and intellectual connection. On January 1, 1994, Melinda and Bill were married in Hawaii. But only a few months later heartbreak struck Bill Gates as his mother succumbed to breast cancer, passing away that June. Gates was devastated.

Bill and Melinda took some time off in 1995 to travel to several countries and get a new perspective on life and the world. In 1996, their first daughter, Jennifer, was born. A year later, Gates moved his family into a 55,000-s□uare-foot, $54-million house on the shore of Lake Washington. Though the house serves as a business center, it is said to be a very cozy home for the couple and their three children. (Their son, Rory, was born in 1999, and a second daughter, Phoebe, arrived in 2002.)

Philanthropic Efforts

With Melinda's influence, Gates took an interest in filling his mother's role as a civic leader. He began to realize that he had an obligation to give more of his wealth to charity. Being the consummate student he was, Gates studied the philanthropic work of Andrew Carnegie and John D. Rockefeller, titans of the American industrial revolution. In 1994, Gates and his wife established the William H. Gates Foundation, which was dedicated to supporting education, world health and investment in low-income communities. In 2000, the couple combined several family foundations to form the Bill & Melinda Gates Foundation. They started out by making a $28 billion contribution to set up the foundation.

Bill Gates stepped down from the day-to-day operations of Microsoft in 2000, turning over the job of CEO to college friend Steve Ballmer, who had been with Microsoft since 1980. He positioned himself as chief software architect so he could concentrate on what was for him the more passionate side of the business, though he remained chairman of the board.

Over the next few years, his involvement with the Bill & Melinda Gates Foundation occupied much of his time and even more of his interest. In 2006, Gates announced he was transitioning himself from full-time work at Microsoft to devote more quality time to the foundation. His last full day at Microsoft was June 27, 2008.

In addition to all the accolades of being one of the richest and most successful businessmen in the history of the world, Bill Gates has also received numerous awards for philanthropic work. Time magazine named Gates one of the most influential people of the 20th century. The magazine also named Gates, his wife Melinda and rock band U2's lead singer, Bono, as the 2005 Persons of the Year.

Gates holds several honorary doctorates from universities throughout the world and an honorary Knight Commander of the Order of the British Empire bestowed by Queen Elizabeth II in 2005. In 2006,

Gates and his wife were awarded the Order of the Aztec Eagle by the Mexican government for their philanthropic work throughout the world in the areas of health and education.

In February 2014, Gates announced that he would be stepping down as chairman of Microsoft in order to move into a new position as technology adviser. In addition to Gates's transition, it was reported that longtime Microsoft CEO Steve Ballmer would be replaced by 46-year-old Satya Nadella.

Gates continues to devote much of his time and energy to the work of the Bill & Melinda Gates Foundation. The organization tackles international and domestic issues, such as health and education. One aspect of its work in the United States is helping students become college ready. In 2015, Gates spoke out in favor of national Common Core standards in grades K through 12 and charter schools.

Gates also proved to be a groundbreaking employer around this time: The foundation announced that it would give its employees a year's paid leave after the birth of a child or the adoption of a child.

In 2016, Gates and his wife Melinda were recognized for their philanthropic work when they were named recipients of the Presidential Medal of Freedom, presented by Barack Obama.

CHAPTER 2- EDUCATION AND MARRIAGE

William Henry Gates III was born in Seattle, Washington on October 28th, 1955. Bills father Bill Gates Jr. worked for a Seattle law firm and Bills mother Mary, taught school until they started their family. Bills parents were married in 1951 and two years later gave birth to their first child, Bills older sister, Kristanne. Two years after that Bill was born and in 1964 the third and final Gates was born, her name is Libby. As a child Bill enjoyed rocking back and forth, today he still has a habit of rocking when he is thinking about something. Bill was very bored at school and his parents knew it so they were always trying to feed him more information to keep him busy. Bills parents finally decided to put him in a private school where he would be challenged more. The Lakeside private school had just bought a new computer when Bill arrived and he was immediately hooked. Within a week he had surpassed the knowledge of the computer teacher at Lakeside. Learning the BASIC programming language was a breeze for Bill and he was soon writing his own programs. Bills love for computers and math led him to a new place around his neighborhood that was renting computer time. He got an arrangement with the owners that he would get free computer time if he found things that would make the computer crash. During this time Bill met Paul Allen his business partner for the rest of his life. Together they started a small company called Traf-O-Data, they sold a small computer outfitted with their program that could count traffic for the city. This company wasn't a big success but it did earn the two boys some money as well as good business skills. Bill also wrote a schedule program for his school which he modified a bit to put little Bill Gates in a class full of the prettiest girls in the school. Bill was deemed by his peers and his teachers as the smartest kid on campus. Upon graduating from Lakeside Bill enrolled in Harvard University in 1973, one of the best universities in the country. Bill was also bored here so he spent most of his time programming, playing poker and seeing how little work he could do and still get A's. He told his teachers that he would be a millionaire by the time he was 30, this was one of the few times he underestimated himself, Bill was a billionaire when he was 31. One of Bills teachers was quoted saying "He was a helluva good programmer, but he's an obnoxious human being." The intense lifestyle Bill lived during his first year in Harvard made him ill for most of the summer of 1974. Bill soon left Harvard for business opportunities in programming which turned him into a multi-billionaire. Later he met Melinda French who he married and they now have a little daughter named Jennifer. It's very interesting that even with all that money Bill drives himself to work in an average family car and he even flies coach. A very interesting man and a very interesting childhood.

How he met melinda,his wife

In summer 1986, freshly graduated from Duke University with a degree in computer science and economics, Melinda Ann French was working as an intern for IBM. She told a recruiter she had one more interview – with a new company called Microsoft. The recruiter was keen. "If you get a job offer from them," she said, "take it because the chance for advancement there is terrific."

Indeed. Six-and-a-half years later, Melinda Ann had advanced through the company, from software marketing tyro to general manager of information products such as Expedia and Encarta; more significantly, she had advanced to a senior role in the heart of the chief executive, Bill Gates, soon to become the world's richest man. Today, she is one half of the world's top charity foundation, with personal jurisdiction over the spending of $80bn (£40bn). Clever, raven-haired, strong-featured and tough as nails, she brings e☐ual amounts of compassion, common sense and business nous to the small matter of alleviating world sickness and poverty.

Born in 1964, she grew up in Dallas, Texas, the daughter of Ray French, an engineer and house-rentals agent. At school, Melinda was earnest, driven and goal-orientated. Her introduction to the cyber-world came at 14 when her father brought home an Apple II, one of the first consumer computers available. She was soon playing computer games, and learning the Basic programming language.

It has always amused Bill Gates that his wife is better educated than him – he is America's most famous college drop-out. They met in 1987, four months into her job at Microsoft, when they sat next to each other at an Expo trade-fair dinner in New York. "He was funnier than I expected him to be," she reported, neutrally. Months went by before, meeting her in the Microsoft car park, he asked her out – in two weeks' time. She said, "ask me nearer the time." He had to explain to her the ceaseless daily flood of meetings.

Whatever first attracted Ms French to Bill Gates, he was struck by her forthrightness and independence. It was she who first spurred him into impulses of charity. After their engagement in 1993, during Melinda's "wedding shower", her mother Mary, suffering from breast cancer, read her an admonitory letter whose gist was, "from those to whom much is given, much is expected". Mary died months later, but her advice provoked the William H Gates Foundation. Run by Bill's father, its aim was to put laptops in every classroom. Then the couple decided that the most pressing issue in the US was reforming the education system.

Then, after their wedding in Hawaii (on New Year's Day 1994) Melinda read in The New York Times about the millions of children in developing countries dying of malaria and TB. She made world poverty their priority concern.

Melinda now spends 30 hours a week on foundation work, as she and Bill assess the charity presentations that flood in. Of the 6,000 re□uests the foundation receives each year, they read only the ones asking for $40m or more. "We go down the chart of the greatest ine□uities, and give where we can effect the greatest change," she told Forbes magazine, in a tone that suggests she doesn't regard it as rocket science. The foundation also links up with other charities and companies like Glaxo on more ambitious projects – like the Global Alliance for Vaccines and Immunisations, which kicked off with donations of $1.5m from each of 17 governments.

It's hard to keep sight of the woman behind the world's top charity: the high-achieving schoolgirl who loved complicated jigsaws and once scaled the 14,000ft Mount Rainier with ropes and crampons; the mother of three; and the devout Catholic who visited Calcutta to talk to Aids sufferers in Mother Teresa's Home for the Dying. But it's clear that the Foundation needs her clarity and good sense. Time magazine, when it put Bill Gates and Bono on the cover as "Person[s] of the Year," included Melinda Gates because she is the heart, as well as the brains, of the organisation. "Lots of people like Bill – and I include myself – are enraged," said Bono, "and we sweep ourselves into a fury at the wanton loss of lives. We need a much slower pulse to help us to be rational. Melinda is that pulse."

CHAPTER 3- BILL GATES AND STEVE JOBS RELATIONSHIP

Looking back at Steve Jobs' tenure at Apple, it's impossible to separate the role Microsoft and Bill Gates played. The companies helped pioneer the industry and define an era. The two CEOs partnered at various times, competed all the time, and challenged one another in ways that helped shape the landscape of technology. It's a complex relationship – which you can witness in this amusing video compilation of Steve Jobs best □uotes about Microsoft.

Let's look a little deeper into the history of this two great men.

Friends (1981 to 1983)

During the development of the Macintosh in the early 80s, Microsoft was an important ally. Apple needed groundbreaking software for it's upcoming platform and Microsoft was one of the few companies developing for it. It was a crucial phase for Apple.

The strength of their relationship could be witnessed at an Internal Apple Event in Hawai where Steve Jobs introduced the Macintosh to a few Apple VIPs. Bill Gates sugarcoated the Mac and Steve Jobs loved every moment of it.

Steve Jobs and Bill Gates were so close at the time that according to a Guardian source, they even double-dated occasionally.

But all good things must end.

Rivals (1983 to 1996)

Steve Jobs had this dream where Apple would dominate the computer business and Microsoft would own the application-side of that business. The OS would naturally also by controlled by Apple.

But Bill Gates wasn't blind. He understood that the Graphical User Interface was the future of computing. He also knew that it would quickly make its DOS operating system irrelevant and threatens Microsoft to become (just) a software company dependent of Apple. Bill Gates had bigger plans.

For years, Microsoft had engineers secretly copying the Macintosh OS and working on its own version of a Graphical OS: Windows. Not long after the Internal Event in Hawaii, Steve Jobs learned the crushing news. Microsoft wanted to compete with Apple; Bill Gates deceived him.

For the next 15 years, Apple would engage in a strange relationship with Microsoft. On one end, Microsoft was prying marketshare away from Apple, on the other, it was one of its biggest partner. Steve Jobs would soon leave Apple and create NeXT but would not succeed to make a dent in Microsoft's dominance.

Along the way, Jobs often sparred with Microsoft, criticizing the company's lack of creativity.

"The only problem with Microsoft is they just have no taste," Jobs said in the 1996 public television documentary "Triumph of the Nerds." "They have absolutely no taste. And I don't mean that in a small way, I mean that in a big way, in the sense that they don't think of original ideas, and they don't bring much culture into their products."

In a New York Times article that ran after the documentary aired, Jobs disclosed that he called Gates afterward to apologize. But only to a degree.

"I told him I believed every word of what I'd said but that I never should have said it in public," Jobs told the Times. "I wish him the best, I really do. I just think he and Microsoft are a bit narrow. He'd be a broader guy if he had dropped acid once or gone off to an ashram when he was younger."

Truce (1997 to 2002)

Things changed when Steve Jobs came back at Apple in 1997. On the brink of bankruptcy, Jobs turned to his 'old ac□uaintance' Bill Gates for help.

The Microsoft Deal is considered a low point in Apple's history by many.

When Steve Jobs announced that Microsoft was not the enemy anymore, few could believe their ears. He went as far as praising the quality of their Mac apps like Office and Internet Explorer... that was outrageous!

Things were weird for a few years – 5 years to be exact. Which corresponds to the 5 years of the 'Microsoft Deal'. During that period Steve Jobs only had good things to say about Redmond. But it was an illusion. If Bill Gates was a great liar, Steve Jobs was his e☐ual.

Frenemies (2003 to 2011)

It's now 2003 and iPods are selling like hotcakes. The Apple brand is cool again.

Apple understood it could not compete with Microsoft on the desktop so it brought the battle to another field: mobile. Here, Microsoft is a minor player. Apple doesn't need Microsoft like it did at the turn of the millenium. So Steve doesn't have to play nice anymore.

Apple's tone of voice about Redmond suddenly changes.

The Get Mac campaign hits the airwaves and pokes fun of the PC industry and Microsoft (watch this All Things D interview with Steve Jobs and Bill Gates were Bill is compared to the PC guy!).

The praising days are over.

Was Steve Jobs still bitter at Bill Gates and Microsoft after all these years?

Steve's sudden change of attitude towards Microsoft in the mid-00s seems to indicate that.

There's however an event that is even more striking. During All Things D5 in 2007, Steve Jobs and Bill Gates were 'finally' reunited on a stage. Steve was given the opportunity to praise Bill Gates when asked what Bill's contribution to the PC industry was. Steve's answer was rather generic: "Bill was the first to truly see the value of software." That's all.

But if Steve was still bitter about Bill, why would he keep a letter of Bill next to his bed during his last moments?

Though to say…

What both men really thought of each others or what really happened behind the curtain will probably never be known. You have to hope that these titans truly shared mutual respects and eventually found grounds to appreciate each others.

Bill Gates statement at the passing of Steve Jobs

I'm truly saddened to learn of Steve Jobs' death. Melinda and I extend our sincere condolences to his family and friends, and to everyone Steve has touched through his work.

Steve and I first met nearly 30 years ago, and have been colleagues, competitors, and friends over the course of more than half our lives.

The world rarely sees someone who has had the profound impact Steve has had, the effects of which will be felt for many generations to come.

For those of us lucky enough to get to work with him, it's been an insanely great honor. I will miss Steve immensely.

CHAPTER 4- BILL GATES INVENTIONS- TOP-GREATEST HITS AND MISSES

Internet Explorer (IE)

Introduced 1995

It's really easy to simply remember "Internet Exploder" as the standards-breaking, web-forking, buggy, monopoly-causing app that helped shape Bill's old image as the evilest baron of all technology companies. But it's also the app that led to the creation Ajax-based web apps through the XMLHttpRe□uest spec, and the kludgey early popularization of CSS. Love it or hate it, IE's gotten more people on the web over the years than any browser, and that's definitely got to count for something.

Media Center

Introduced 2002

Despite TiVo's DVR dominance and competitors that came and went over the years, Media Center has always been an underrated standout product. Even Bill admits that the company's long struggled with usability, but Media Center is a beacon of hope not only for 10-foot UIs everywhere, but also for the company's ability to create powerful, advanced, user-friendly products. Between its online integration, extensible plugin architecture, ability to stream shows to nodes around the house, and now CableCARD support, the only real downside to Media Center is the fact that you still need a full-blown PC to run it.

MS-DOS

Introduced 1981, discontinued 2000

It was arcane and nigh-unusable to mere mortals -- but the early cash-cow was one of Bill's most strategic moves, and helped Microsoft define the concept of software licensing. It also helped launched Mossberg's career as crusader of user-friendly technology. But most importantly, MS-DOS was still the OS an entire generation grew up learning, so del criticism.* for a second because our autoexec.bat and config.sys were so very well crafted, and extensively tweaking Memmaker for a few extra KB of usable RAM definitely ranks amongst our top most formative geek moments.

Office

Introduced 1989 (on Mac), 1990 (on PC)

Word, Excel and PowerPoint certainly did well enough on their own, but when Microsoft combined 'em into the tidy (and pricey) package that is Office -- first on the Mac in 1989, interestingly -- it had a selling point that would prove irresistible to many a productivity-obsessed middle manager even today. The addition of Outlook and it's support for the (for some) nigh-indispensable Exchange only further solidified its foothold in the corporate computing world, and that's where Bill knew the real money was. That's certainly not to say that it hasn't been without its share of problems and annoyances, though -- we're looking at you, Clippy.

Peripherals

Introduced 1982

Microsoft has always been a software company first, but it's been cranking out high-□uality peripherals for over 25 years -- long before the Xbox and Zune were even a twinkle in Bill's eye. Not only that, but it's been a reliable innovator in the field, with a string of devices that were first, early, or just simply popularized technologies like the wheel mouse, force-feedback joysticks and controllers, the modern optical mouse, and the ergo-keyboard. The division has gone through some bumpy times -- the SideWinder line was killed off for a while there, and there've been some □uestionable designs along the way -- but it's been riding high as of late, and it doesn't show any signs of slowing down soon.

Windows 3.1 / NT 3.5

Introduced 1992 and 1994

It took a few versions to come into its own, but by the time Windows hit 3.1, Microsoft finally had a product that was able to pull PC users away from the command line (for some of the time, at least) and give them a real taste of things to come. Windows NT may not have had quite the same appeal with the average consumer, but it did bring the operating system into the 32-bit world and pave the way for enterprise desktop computing as we know it today. (Plus, it had the NT file system (NTFS), which to this day continues to carry on the legacy in its own little way.) We really wish they'd made a sequel to the Pirates of Silicon Valley, because we'd love to have seen the dramatization of Bill overseeing the first popularized versions of Windows -- especially '95, which came out just a couple of years later.

Windows 2000 and XP

Introduced 2000

When thinking of Microsoft and the new millennium, few people are able to keep the crinkles out of their nose. Thankfully, Windows ME wasn't the only thing that arrived in late Y2K, as Windows 2000 rushed in to rock the socks off of suits everywhere. The whole Win2K thing went over so well that Gates and company decided to base its next consumer OS, XP, off of it. Some may argue that the resulting product still stands as the last great OS to ship out of Redmond.

Windows CE / Mobile

Introduced 1996

As two of the most ubi☐uitous projects to come out from under Bill's command, both Windows CE and Windows Mobile are almost impossible to avoid when it comes to handhelds or phones. What began as a mishmash of small components has grown into the adaptable -- though sometimes maddening -- mobile OS that resides on just about every kind of device you can think of. Really, we mean every kind of device, from PMPs to enterprise-level stock-keeping systems. The slimmed down and restructured micro-Windows is at the very least one of the more flexible offerings the company has ever produced. Say what you will about its usability, there's no denying the massive impact it's had on portability and convergence.

Xbox and Xbox 360

Introduced 2001 and 2005

Back in 1999, Bill was all about multimedia convergence, and he said that a new gaming / multimedia device would be Microsoft's trojan horse into the world's living rooms with something coined the "DirectX-box." In 2001, the original Xbox entered gaming territory dominated by Sony's PlayStation with Nintendo's N64. But the clunky machine brought with it the first easy to use multiplayer console service, Xbox Live, as well as a developer-centric model that helped turn the tables. Of course, things look quite a bit different today: the Xbox 360 leads the former market leader's PlayStation 3 in spend and attach rate, and with the relative success of media and content sales on Xbox Live, it seems Bill's dream of dominating the living room wasn't just a pipe-dream after all.

Visual Basic

Introduced 1991, discontinued 1998

It's hard to underestimate the impact of Visual Basic. While the average user might have never heard of the original VB that Microsoft released way back when, the simplicity of the language and its graphical toolset made just about any power user a potential app developer, powering the flood of third party application development Microsoft operating systems enjoyed throughout the 90's. Sadly, Visual Basic met its demise at the hands of more modern languages and toolsets, but with a legacy of making programming accessible to the masses, its place in the history books and in Bill's pocketbook is undoubtedly secure.

Misses

Auto PC

Introduced 1998, discontinued 2001

Riding high on its previously-introduced sister products -- the Handheld PC and Palm PC platforms, now dead and transformed into Windows Mobile, respectively -- Microsoft's Auto PC initiative was promised to herald a revolution for in-car entertainment and productivity. There's no question it was well ahead of its time; in fact, many of the features debuted in Auto PC have gone on to become standard fare in today's cars. Problem was when it launched your ride was already pimped with a mere CD player. In-car navigation, voice recognition, and MP3 support were still the stuff of science fiction in those dark days (particularly at the four-digit asking price), and the whole thing was doomed to a geeky, spendy niche. Though products were initially expected from several manufacturers, Clarion ended up being the only one to actually produce a head unit.

*The Auto PC lived on in spirit as Clarion's Joyride, but Microsoft's heart was no longer in the project and Clarion had switched to a generic Windows CE-based core to build the product.

Microsoft Bob

Introduced 1995, discontinued 1996

Poor Bob. No one ever gave him a chance. Maybe it had to do with the fact that he was really annoying. And as it turns out, Bill was dating Melinda French, Bob's program manager. Which isn't to say there was any nepotism involved -- Bob suffered an early death in 1996 due to general hatred for the little bastard. Bill offered this to a column in January 1997, "Unfortunately, [Bob] demanded more performance than typical computer hardware could deliver at the time and there wasn't an ade□uately large market. Bob died." Thankfully, Billinda's blossoming relationship lived on. Oh, did you hear? They're like the world's greatest philanthropists now.

Cairo

Introduced 1991 (but never released)

Ask folks to pick one word to describe Microsoft's technology roadmap in the 1990s and you'll commonly get "Cairo" in response. Announced before Windows NT 3.1 was even released, Cairo was occasionally an operating system, occasionally a collection of new technologies -- it depended entirely upon who and when you asked -- but at its core, it was intended to guide Microsoft on the path beyond the architecture introduced by NT. After throwing countless dollars and man-hours at the ambitious project, Cairo was ultimately canned (though mentions of the storied buzzword continued even into this decade). Although Windows 2000 eventually became NT's heir apparent, the fruits of Microsoft's labor weren't entirely for naught, as various Cairo features found themselves implanted into various versions of Windows throughout the years. Even the WinFS file system can trace its roots back to the project -- fitting, because it too has become such an albatross.

MSN Music and URGE

Introduced 2004 and 2006, both fully discontinued 2008

When MSN Music -- Microsoft's effort to build its own PlaysForSure-based subscription music based store -- imploded, headstrong Bill did what he usually does: rebrand and launch again. When he got up at CES 2006 and announced MSN Music would become URGE with MTV, we were all a little skeptical -- after all, the problem wasn't really the service, it was the overbearing DRM and the fact that consumers simply weren't ready for subscription music. Of course, eventually URGE died as well, and MTV shunted customers to Rhapsody America; naturally, Microsoft had a third PlaysForSure-based store waiting in the wings with Zune, which doesn't appear to be going anywhere any time soon.

Origami / UMPC

Introduced 2006

UMPCs... what can we say? Sure, Scoble liked them, but even from day one we never saw the market potential. Fueled by an early and too-successful hype-generating viral campaign of Microsoft's own making, there was no way that these first generation Origami devices would achieve their promise. Overpriced, underpowered, desktop OS-laden (with Microsoft's Touch Pack add-on), and poor battery life all helped ensure drown UMPCs in the wave of "ultramobile lifestyle PC"-hysteria they rode to market. And as UMPCs begin to fade, the shrinking niche between smartphones and laptops can look forward to the sweet release of MIDs -- though that's already been two years... and counting.

OS/2

Dates: introduced 1987, discontinued 2006

What began as a collaboration between Microsoft and then-partner IBM blossomed into what looked like -- for a time at least -- the logical successor to the DOS / Windows empire. The advanced OS showed early signs of greatness with it's incorporation of the HPFS file system, improved networking capabilities, and a sophisticated UI. But cracks in the relationship between the two powerhouse corporations would ultimately lead to its downfall. With Windows 3 a sudden success, IBM's reluctance to go hardware neutral, and Microsoft's increasing displeasure with code which it called "bloated" (ahem!), the project was eventually swept aside by Gates and the gang to make way for what would become the omnipresent operating system you know and love and/or hate today.

SPOT watches and MSN Direct

Introduced 2004, discontinued 2008

When the concept of an information-enabled watch that automagically received content over unused FM radio subcarriers was first conjured up by Microsoft in the early part of the decade, it seemed like a fabulous idea. So much so, in fact, Bill personally took the project under his wing. But by the time it had launched, it was already doomed by a perfect storm of problems: the devices were uglier than sin and comically oversized, the bizarre ad campaign featured frighteningly hairy cartoon arms, and -- as the mobile web was just starting to pick up steam at that time -- virtually anyone who would've been interested in that kind of product had already discovered ways to get the same information from their phone. The underlying data network Microsoft built out to support the watches, MSN Direct, lives on to this day and sees plenty of use in Garmin's nüvi line, but will it ever be used to beam weather, news, and MSFT stock reports to wrists other than Bill's? Not bloody likely.

Windows Activation

Introduced 2001

Depending on who you talk to, Windows Product Activation is a serious privacy violation, a headache, minimal protection against piracy, or all of the above. Lucky for us, Microsoft is finally seeing (some of) the folly of its overbearing ways and has gone with a more permissive nagware method with Vista SP1. This as opposed to the regular method of routinely locking users out of their systems, which, would not you know it, tended to hurt legitimate users more than pirates. Perhaps the best example of Windows Activation's legacy was the great WGA outage of 2007, which left 12,000 systems out in the cold due to few downed servers at Microsoft. It didn't take long for the servers to bounce back, but any shred of reputation the service had at that point went out the window with the uptime.

Windows ME

Introduced September 2000

It's not exactly clear what the point of Windows Millennium Edition was -- our guess is that Microsoft needed to keep up with that year-based product naming scheme it had going at the time, and cranked out this half-baked update to '98 in order to capitalize on the turn-of-the-millennium frenzy. Unlike the NT-based Windows 2000 released at the same time, Windows ME retained its MS-DOS-based core while managing to somehow get even more slow and unstable than its predecessors 95 and 98. And to add insult to injury, it restricted access to shell mode, rendering many MS-DOS apps incompatible. Thankfully, Windows ME was only inflicted upon consumers for little over a year; it was replaced by indomitable Windows XP in 2001.

Windows Vista
Introduced 2007

Vista doesn't suck. Let's just get that off our chests. In fact, it's a □uite capable, secure and sexy OS when you get right down to it. Unfortunately, its problems just loomed too large for many folks to overlook. A multitude of delays and a rapidly diminishing feature list soured people right out of the gate, and once the dust settled people just weren't happy with the minor improvements they were getting in exchange for their hard-earned monies and fairly mandatory RAM upgrades. Mix that in with the standard driver incompatibilities of any Microsoft OS upgrade, and you've got a whole bunch of disgruntled downgraders on your hands -- and plenty of bad press to fill in any remaining gaps. Sadly, improvements to Media Center, aesthetics and even that □uirky little sidebar got overlooked in the process. Microsoft's already scrambling to get Windows 7 together to capture the multitude of users that have decided to skip Vista altogether, let's just hope it's not too late.

CHAPTER 5- THINGS YOU DON'T KNOW ABOUT BILL GATES

What are the first three things that come to your mind when you hear the name 'Bill Gates'?

1. He's the richest man in the world with a net worth of $79 billion.

2. He is the co-founder of Microsoft, the world's largest and most successful PC software company.

3. He is the world's most prolific humanitarian who donates generously through the Bill & Melinda Gates Foundation.

Besides his philanthropic efforts and online presence, there are lot of things about Gates that you probably didn't know. While there are many unknown facts about Gates, we bring to you the top 15 surprising facts about him:

1. Born as William Henry Gates III, Bill's nickname as a child was "Trey," reflective of The Third" following his moniker, as he was the fourth consecutive Gates man of the same name.

2. Gates wrote his first computer program on a General Electric computer as a young teenager at Lakeside Prep School. It was a version of tic-tac-toe, where you could play against the computer.

3. Once his school discovered Gates' coding abilities, they let him write the school's computer program for scheduling students in classes. Apparently, he slyly altered the code so that he would get placed in classes with mostly female students.

4. Gates scored 1590 out of 1600 on his SATs.

5. Gates, Paul Allen and Paul Gilbert launched a company while Gates and Allen were still students at Lakeside School in Seattle. Their Traf-O-Data 8008 computer was designed to read data from roadside traffic counters and create reports for traffic engineers.

6. Gates was a college dropout. He left Harvard University in 1975 to fully devote himself to Microsoft.

7. Gates was arrested in New Mexico in 1977, for jumping a red-light and driving without a licence.

8. Bill Gates aimed to become a millionaire by the age of 30. However, he became a billionaire at 31.

9. At Microsoft, Gates used to memorize employees' license plates to keep tabs on their comings and goings. "Eventually I had to loosen up, as the company got to a reasonable size," he said.

10. In 1994, he was asked by a TV interviewer if he could jump over a chair from a standing position. Gates promptly took the challenge and leaped over the chair like a boss.

11. One of Gates' biggest splurges was the Codex Leicester, a collection of writings by Leonardo da Vinci. He ac□uired it at 1994 auction for $30.8 million.

12. He flew coach until 1997, even though his net worth was already well into the double-digit billions.

13. Despite his immense wealth, Gates doesn't believe in leaving children a ton of money as inheritance; his three kids (daughters Jennifer and Phoebe and son Rory) will inherit only $10 million each — just a fraction of his $81.1 billion net worth. "Leaving kids massive amounts of money is not a favor to them," he says.

14. Gates says that if Microsoft had not worked out, he probably would've been a researcher for artificial intelligence.

15. Gates doesn't know any foreign languages, which he says is his biggest regret in life so far.

CONCLUSION

Humanity's greatest advances are not in its discoveries, but in how those discoveries are applied to reduce ine□uity." – Bill Gates

Passion, intensity, and tenacity.   That's one way to describe Bill Gates.

Leave the World a Better Place Than You Found It

He fights the good fight to leave the world a better place than he found it, and he's a worldwide giver of epic proportions. In fact, he and Warren Buffet joined forces to drive a campaign to encourage the wealthiest people to give most of their money to philanthropic causes (see The Giving Pledge.)

Create Systems and Ecosystems to Change the World

It's one thing to be smart. It's another thing to be resourceful. It's yet another thing to get results. Bill Gates is a visionary that makes things happen by creating systems bigger than himself and inspiring people to join him on epic adventures to change the world. He's not a seeker of fame or a seeker of fortune, although he has both. He's a maker of impact. Technology is his way, and reducing ine□uities in the world is his game.

Who better to learn some lessons for life than from a master of the game of life? With that in mind, let's see what lessons we can borrow from Bill Gates' playbook.

25 Lessons Learned from Bill Gates

Bill is full of lessons and insights. Here are 25 plays we can take from the pages of his playbook:

1. Change the world, or go home.

There is a little sign on many doors at Microsoft. It features the blue monster and it reads: "Change the world, or go home." Not only does that phrase capture the spirit of thousands of Softies ... it speaks to the way Bill Gates drives his life. He lives to build a better world, whether it's one version, one platform, one system, one idea, one cause, one innovation at a time. The beauty is, he knows how to scale and amplify his impact in powerful ways – he's on top of his game.

2. Blaze the trail.

The path isn't always there. Sometimes you have to make it. Sometimes people will think you're crazy. Sometimes you are just ahead of the curve. it's a dream for a reason, and sometimes making your dreams happen takes going out on a limb and giving your all for what you believe in. Bill Gates believed that the personal computer was the future and that there should be one on every desktop and in the living room and it would change the way we work and how we live in unimaginable ways.

3. Make an impact.

Drive from impact. Bill Gates makes choices based on impact. Whether it's following his passion or investing in a cause, he drives from making impact. He doesn't just do things because he can. He does things because they matter and he can make them scale.

4. Humanities greatest advances are the ones that level the playing field.

Bill Gates has a strong belief that "All lives have e□ual value." Help those that can't help themselves. Everybody deserves a chance at their best life. Lift the underdogs of the world up. In his speech at Harvard, Bill says, "Taking a look back, one big re□ret is, I left Harvard with no real awareness of the awful inequities in the world. The appalling disparities of health and wealth and opportunity that condemned millions of people to the lives of despair. I learned a lot here at Harvard about new ideas and economics, and politics. I got great exposure to the advances being made in the sciences. But humanities greatest advances are not in its discoveries, but in how those discoveries are applied to reduce inequity."

5. A sense of urgency.

The world changes fast. The market changes faster. Bill says, "In this business, by the time you realize you're in trouble, it's too late to save yourself. Unless you're running scared all the time, you're gone."

6. The market doesn't always drive the right things.

In one of his powerful TED talks, Bill says, "There are some very important problems that don't get worked on naturally. That is the market does not drive the scientists, the communicators, the thinkers, the government to do the right things. And only by paying attention to these things, and having brilliant people who care and draw other people in, can we make as much progress as we need to." Watch TED – Bill Gates on Mos☐uitos, Malaria, and Education.

7. Live your values.

When you let the world know what you're about, you become a lightening rod and you attract people with the same values. At Microsoft, Bill Gates attracted people with a passion for changing the world and joining him on a journey to help create better lives through technology and innovation. On the philanthropy side, Gates connects with U2's Bono beyond the music when it comes to sharing their global mission to end poverty, disease, and indifference. In 2005, TIME named Bono, Bill and Melinda Gates, "Persons of the Year" for their humanitarian work. On Bill Gate's 54'th birthday, Bono had this to say before leading the crowd in Happy Birthday: "Without him, and without his business, we just wouldn't be where we are today. It's his birthday today. Bill Gates is in the house." Watch Bono Wishes Bill Gates a Happy Birthday.

8. Your best gets better with the right people.

Don't go it alone. You're better when you've got the right people around you. Bill Gates built a culture of the best and brightest and was good at convincing his friends, such as Paul Allen and Steve Ballmer to join him on his adventures. By surrounding himself with smart people, Bill was able to scale. He also had sounding board for ideas. More importantly, ideas could get better from the combined smarts and perspectives. Bill also knows how to complement his strengths by having the right people around that make up for his weaknesses.

9. Innovation is the heart and soul of a business.

It's about bringing ideas to market and applying research. If you don't innovate you die. The world keeps changing. To stay ahead of the game, or even to stay in the game, you have to keep innovating: innovate in your products, innovate in your process, innovate in the markets, etc. Bill Gates uses innovation as a way to drive impact whether it's shaping software or saving the planet.

10. Be the platform.

Be the platform people can build on. See the role that you play in building something that let's other people build on what you do best.

11. Build a better system.

Don't just solve a one-off problem. Make the solution systematic and make it repeatable. Find, create, or leverage systems. There is always a system, whether it's at the micro-level or the macro level. The system has inputs and outputs, cycles, and levers. Whether you're creating the system or leveraging the system, you're more effective when you realize that there is a system.

12. Build an ecosystem.

There are systems and ecosystems all around us. Bill says, "Personal computing today is a rich ecosystem encompassing massive PC-based data centers, notebook and Tablet PCs, handheld devices, and smart cell phones. It has expanded from the desktop and the data center to wherever people need it — at their desks, in a meeting, on the road or even in the air." On creating partners for your ecosystem, Bill says, "Our success has really been based on partnerships from the very beginning."

13. Know how to turn the crank.

Take action. Execute. The problem isn't a shortage of ideas, it's execution. Lots of people have ideas. There is an overload of ideas. The real gap is bringing ideas to market in a way that matters. The secret sauce is ruthless prioritization of the ideas that make the most impact.

14. Take Care of Your People.

Bill Gates says, "Great organizations demand a high level of commitment by the people involved." He set a powerful example of taking care of employees, from private offices for developers to creating a workplace of extreme empowerment, engagement, and passion.

15. Divide and con☐uer the problem.

There is always a way to chunk up the problem and prioritize more effectively. Whether it's slicing the problem into versions over time, or simply taking the most meaningful or highest ROI (Return On Investment) pieces of the problem and tackling them first, you can make progress on the worst of problems or the best of opportunities. No problem withstands sustained, focused effort that learns and improves over time.

16. Improving your odds doesn't guarantee success.

One of Bill's stories during his speech at Harvard is how he learned this lesson: "Radcliff was a great place to live. There were more women up there and most of the guys were mad science types. The combination offered me the best odds if you know what I mean."

17. You do not have to be first to win.

Bill says, "Microsoft has had its success by doing low-cost products and constantly improving those products and we've really redefined the IT industry to be something that's about a tool for individuals."

18. The toughest feedback to hear, is the feedback you need the most.

You get better by listening to your toughest critics. Your greatest source of growth can come from the people that will tell you what you need to hear, not just what you want to hear. Bill says, "Your most unhappy customers are your greatest source of learning." Bill also says, "You've got to want to be in this incredible feedback loop where you get the world-class people to tell you what you're doing wrong."

19. Business and technology go hand in hand.

Bill says, "Information technology and business are becoming inextricably interwoven. I don't think anybody can talk meaningfully about one without the talking about the other." We're truly living a knowledge worker world, where information technology is front and center. Bill says, "It's pretty incredible to look back 30 years to when Microsoft was starting and realize how work has been transformed. We're finally getting close to what I call the digital workstyle."

20. Frame the problem.

Bill says, "I believe that if you show people the problems and you show them the solutions they will be moved to act." Framing a problem is simply how you look at a problem, just like how you frame a picture. It's about choosing what to focus on, what's in and what's out. When you frame the problem, you bound it. Framing also helps you get a better perspective on the problem, as well as share the problem more effectively with others. Some questions to help frame a problem include: Who's the customer? What are their needs and priorities? What's happening in the market? What are competitors doing? What are our options for responding? How do we differentiate? How is technology changing and what possibilities does it offer our customers? What are the priorities for our business?

21. Celebrate success, but learn from failure.

Don't repeat the same mistakes and don't wallow in your wins. Bill says, ""It's fine to celebrate success but it is more important to heed the lessons of failure."

22. Technology is just a tool.

Don't lose sight of the end in mind or the difference that makes the difference. Bill says, "Technology is just a tool. In terms of getting the kids working together and motivating them, the teacher is the most important."

23. Don't automate inefficiency.

Make sure something actually makes sense to automate, otherwise you compound the problem. Bill says, "The first rule of any technology used in a business is that automation applied to an efficient operation will magnify the efficiency. The second is that automation applied to an inefficient operation will magnify the inefficiency."

24. Empower people.

Put the right information into the hands of the people that can make the most of it. Bill says, ""The vision is really about empowering workers, giving them all the information about what's going on so they can do alot more than they've done in the past."

25. Go digital.

Connect people, process, and technology. Create a digital landscape or a virtual world to reduce friction and to create new possibilities. Bill says, ""One of the wonderful things about the information highway is that virtual equity is far easier to achieve than real-world e□uity…We are all created equal in the virtual world and we can use this equality to help address some of the sociological problems that society has yet to solve in the physical world."

Bill Gates death hoax spreads on Facebook

Rumors of the business man's alleged demise gained traction on Tuesday after a 'R.I.P. Bill Gates' Facebook page attracted nearly one million of 'likes'. Those who read the 'About' page were given a believable account of the American business man's passing:

"At about 11 a.m. ET on Tuesday (June 06, 2017), our beloved business man Bill Gates passed away. Bill Gates was born on October 28, 1955 in Seattle. He will be missed but not forgotten. Please show your sympathy and condolences by commenting on and liking this page."

Hundreds of fans immediately started writing their messages of condolence on the Facebook page, expressing their sadness that the talented 61-year-old business man was dead. And as usual, Twittersphere was frenzied over the death hoax.

Where as some trusting fans believed the post, others were immediately skeptical of the report, perhaps learning their lesson from the huge amount of fake death reports emerging about celebrities over recent months. Some pointed out that the news had not been carried on any major American network, indicating that it was a fake report, as the death of a business man of Bill Gates' stature would be major news across networks.

A recent poll conducted for the Celebrity Post shows that a large majority (94%) of respondents think those Bill Gates death rumors are not funny anymore.

Bill Gates Death Hoax Dismissed Since Business man Is 'Alive And Well'

On Wednesday (June 07) the business man's reps officially confirmed that Bill Gates is not dead. "He joins the long list of celebrities who have been victimized by this hoax. He's still alive and well, stop believing what you see on the Internet," they said.

Some fans have expressed anger at the fake report saying it was reckless, distressing and hurtful to fans of the much loved business man. Others say this shows his extreme popularity across the globe.

Top 10 Bill Gates' Quotes

Here are my top 10 favorite Bill Gates' □uotes:

"As we look ahead into the next century, leaders will be those who empower others."

"If you give people tools, and they use their natural ability and their curiosity, they will develop things in ways that will surprise you very much beyond what you might have expected."

"If you show people the problems and you show people the solutions they will be moved to act."

"In terms of doing things, I take a fairly scientific approach to why things happen and how they happen."

"Never before in history has innovation offered promise of so much to so many in so short a time."

"Often you have to rely on intuition."

"Success is a lousy teacher. It seduces smart people into thinking they can't lose."

"It's fine to celebrate success but it is more important to heed the lessons of failure."

"You've got to want to be in this incredible feedback loop where you get the world-class people to tell you what you're doing wrong."

"Your most unhappy customers are your greatest source of learning."

Printed in Great Britain
by Amazon